PREFACE

THE FOLLOWING LECTURE was prepared at the request of the Theological Institute of Bucharest, and delivered there on 18 January 1977. It was originally given in French, and in a somewhat shortened version, on account of the need for translation into Romanian.

It is always a challenge, and in some ways a daunting one, to try to speak on behalf of one's own Church and people in the midst of a Church with a very different historical experience, living in a very different contemporary situation. The length and quality of the discussion which followed the lecture encouraged me to feel that what had been said had indeed been heard across the barriers of language and culture, and had evoked a warm and interested response. How these pages will be received by my fellow-Anglicans is another question, and one in its own way no less daunting.

For those of us from abroad who received the degree of Doctor *honoris causa* in the course of those January days, our stay in Bucharest was necessarily a moving experience; doubly so, because the Romanian Orthodox Church had decided to take the occasion to pay a tribute of affection and gratitude to the man who for almost thirty years had been its leader and inspiration, the late Patriarch Justinian. At a special meeting of the Holy Synod held on Sunday 16 January, at which we were privileged to be present, he too received the degree of Doctor *honoris causa*. We could not at that time know that the Patriarch was so near the end of his life, though his physical frailty was evident to all. The vision of that great and good man, radiant in and through his frailty, will not easily be forgotten. It testified in a way beyond words to the manifestation of God's glory in and through the weakness and limitations of earth, the very theme of this lecture.

A. M. ALLCHIN

Canterbury, October 1977

TRINITY AND INCARNATION IN ANGLICAN TRADITION

IN ACCEPTING THE HONOUR you have done me in conferring a doctoral degree, and reflecting on the meaning of this gesture, it seemed to me that it might be appropriate to attempt to give some account of the distinctive theological tradition of the Church to which I belong, and to show, if it is possible, certain constant themes and tendencies which recur in Anglican theology during the last four centuries.

I should like to begin in the present by referring to a book published last year entitled *The Contradiction of Christianity*. It is the work of one of the most creative and profound theologians of our Church, Canon David Jenkins, who was for some years Director of the Humanum Studies at Geneva for the World Council of Churches, and is now Director of the William Temple Foundation in Manchester. It is a book, for a large part, concerned with the vital human and social problems which confront mankind at the present time, and with the varying situations which the Christian faith has to meet in different parts of the world. But it contains within itself chapters of a more directly theological nature, luminous pages for instance on the nature of corporate knowledge as the centre of the Church's tradition, or on the restoration of the image and likeness of God in man. It concludes with a chapter, 'The Trinity—love in the end', in which the underlying reasons for the Church's formulation of its belief in God, Father, Son and Holy Spirit are discussed and expounded, and the living significance of that faith affirmed for today. We see the orthodox formulations of the past not as dead or abstract forms of words, but as living powers for the growth of man's life, personal and social, now and in the future. As David Jenkins puts it: 'The Trinity is a symbol for pilgrims who know no limits to their hopes of endurance, discovery and enjoyment.'[1]

I refer to this book now at the beginning, and I shall refer to it again at the end, because it seems to me to provide a striking example of the continuing vitality of a tradition which can be traced through the centuries since the breaking of communion between our Church and Rome, a tradition which certainly has its roots much earlier than the changes of the sixteenth century.

I

As is well known, the pressures of the State on the Church played a very large part in the English Reformation of the sixteenth century. There was in England at this time no teacher of the power and genius of either Luther or Calvin on the continent of Europe. The particular ability of Thomas Cranmer, the first Reformed Archbishop of Canterbury, was as a liturgist and not as a dogmatic theologian. He gave to our Church its classical formularies of worship in the form of the Book of Common Prayer. The old Latin liturgical tradition was translated into English, the services shortened and adapted so as to allow the people to take an active part in them, and so as to strengthen their scriptural and didactic element. This liturgical tradition, through all its subsequent variations, has remained of primordial importance in forming our distinctive way of living the Christian life and reflecting on the mysteries of the faith. But it was only very gradually in the century following 1558 that a distinctive theological viewpoint emerged within the Church of England. It was not till the middle of the seventeenth century that its outlines had become clearly visible.

Here we have one of the principle reasons for the comparative indistinctness of the Anglican theological position as compared with that of the two main traditions of the continental Reformation. In the case of Luther there grew up from the teaching of the reformer himself a whole vision of the Christian faith centred upon and controlled by the doctrine of justification by faith alone. In the case of Calvin, it was the doctrine of the sovereign and predestinating grace of God which provided the key to an even clearer and more systematic way of expounding the Christian revelation. What theological principle can we find in the Anglicanism of the period to correspond to these great and commanding affirmations of the continental reformers?

To answer this question we shall turn to the two most influential writers of the classical period of our theological literature, Richard Hooker (1554-1600) and Bishop Lancelot Andrewes (1555-1626). But first we must notice a vital point about their theological method. The Anglican reformers were at one with their continental contemporaries over against Rome in affirming the supreme authority of Scripture in establishing the faith. 'Are you persuaded that the Holy Scriptures contain sufficiently all doctrine required of necessity for eternal salvation through faith in Christ

2

Jesus?' the bishop is asked at the time of his consecration. But this principle of the primacy of the Scriptures can be interpreted in many different ways. As they worked out their own position, the Anglican theologians came more and more to rely on the concordant testimony of the teachers of the undivided Church, and in particular on the dogmatic decisions of the first four General Councils, as providing the way of approach to the understanding of Scipture. The authority of Scripture was received in and through the witness of Tradition. Nor was this appeal to the early Church made only in matters of doctrine. In liturgical and canonical matters it was also significant. In the same Office for the Consecration of a Bishop, the archbishop begins his address to the man about to be consecrated, 'Brother, forasmuch as the Holy Scriptures and the ancient Canons command . . .' thus linking the authority of the canons with that of Scripture itself. 'As for my religion,' wrote one of the holiest bishops of our Church at the beginning of the eighteenth century, Thomas Ken, 'I die in the Holy Catholic and Apostolic faith, professed by the whole Church before the disunion of East and West, and more particularly I die in the Communion of the Church of England as it stands distinguished from all papal and puritan innovations.'

Such a way of approach, which puts great weight on the study of the Fathers, naturally leads towards a theology of a patristic kind. If we ask where we may find the central point of the theology of Richard Hooker, we shall go not to the doctrine of justification, nor to the doctrine of grace, but to the doctrine of the Incarnation of the Word of God. By common consent, the most profound section in the whole of his great work, *On the Laws of Ecclesiastical Polity*, occurs in the fifth book where, turning aside from the details of his controversy with the puritans about ceremonies and forms of worship, he steps back in order to consider what it is that all the sacraments and rites of the Church signify and perform:

> Sacraments are the powerful instruments of God to eternal life. For as our natural life consisteth in the union of the body with the soul, so our life supernatural in the union of the soul with God. And forasmuch as there is no union of God with man without that mean between both which is both, it seemeth requisite that we first consider how God is in Christ, then how Christ is in us, and how the sacraments do serve to make us partakers of Christ. In other things we may be more brief, but the weight of these requireth largeness.[2]

With these words Hooker introduces his magisterial exposition of Chalce-donian Christology, making it the basis alike of his understanding of the Church and of the sacraments.

If we are looking for the key concepts in Hooker's theological thought, we shall find them in terms such as mutual participation and conjunction, co-inherence and perichoresis. God is in Christ; Christ is in us; we are in him.

> Life, as all other gifts and benefits, groweth originally from the Father and cometh not to us but by the Son, nor by the Son to any of us in particular but through the Spirit. For this cause the Apostle writeth to the church of Corinth, 'The grace of our Lord Jesus Christ, and the love of God, and the fellowship of the Holy Ghost.' Which three Saint Peter comprehendeth in one, 'The participation of the divine Nature'. . . . The Church is in Christ as Eve was in Adam. Yea by grace we are every one of us in Christ and in his Church, as by nature we are in those our first parents. God made Eve of the rib of Adam. And his Church he formeth out of the very flesh, the very wounded and bleeding side of the Son of man. His body crucified and his blood shed for the life of the world, are the true elements of that heavenly being, which maketh us such as he himself is of whom we come.[3]

It is true that Hooker here avoids the explicit language of *theosis*, but it does not escape our attention that when he speaks of Christ 'making us such as he himself is' he affirms the underlying mystery which the word expresses.

It is one of the misfortunes of the Christian West that until the present century, the thought of Maximus the Confessor has been very little known and appreciated. Hooker was a man of amazingly wide erudition, but he can hardly have known the work of the Confessor. Nevertheless I have often thought that there is a certain similarity between them. In both cases one has a theologian with a gift for drawing together and synthesising many varied strands from the previous tradition; a thinker whose work is marked by great balance and judgement. Above all one who does not seek to enhance the glory of God by minimising or denying the goodness of God's creation, but who sets out the way in which the energies of God work in and through all the diversity of the created order. In his own time, Hooker was involved in resisting the tendency in Calvinist theology to exalt God at the expense of man, grace at the expense of nature. He is concerned to defend the true use of reason, the due claims of human institutions and law. But as a remarkable Christian writer of our own time, C. S. Lewis, remarks, it would be a great mistake to suppose that this means that there is any tendency towards secularising in him. 'Few model universes are more filled—one might say more drenched—with Deity than his. "All things that are of God [and only sin is not], have God in them and he them in himself likewise"; yet "their substance and his wholly differeth." God is unspeakably transcendent; but also unspeakably immanent.' The whole immensely varied world which God has made is seen in all its multiplicity. The various levels of human life have their own 'laws', their own principles of action. Yet in and through them all the unifying energies of God are at work. 'We meet on all levels the divine wisdom shining through "the beautiful variety of all things in their manifold and yet harmonious dissimilitude".'[4]

The balance and proportion which mark the work of Richard Hooker are to be found in a different form in the writings of his younger contemporary, Bishop Lancelot Andrewes. In his case the heart of his theology is to be found not in his controversial writings, the argument with Bellarmine for instance, but in the great series of sermons preached at Christmas, Easter and Whitsun before the royal court in London, where year by year he expounded the mysteries of Christ's birth, death and resurrection and the coming of the Spirit, with amazing erudition and skill. Here we find the depth and power of his exposition of the Church's faith in Father, Son and Holy Spirit, a faith enriched and enlivened by the wealth of his biblical and patristic knowledge. I intend to examine simply one strand of this fabric, his exposition of the doctrine of *theosis* as the consequence and completion of the doctrine of the Incarnation. I quote from a sermon for Pentecost in which he compares the work of Christ with the work of the Holy Spirit:

> These, if we should compare them, it would not be easy to determine, whether is greater of these two: 1) That of the Prophet, *Filius datus est nobis*; or 2) that of the Apostle, *Spiritus datus est nobis*; the ascending of our flesh, or the descending of His Spirit; *incarnatio Dei*, or *inspiratio hominis*; the mystery of his incarnation, or the mystery of our inspiration. For mysteries they are both, and 'great mysteries of godliness' both; and in both of them 'God is manifested in the flesh'. In the former by the union of His Son; in the latter by the communion

5

of his blessed Spirit. But we will not compare them, they are both above all comparison. Yet this we may safely say of them: without either of them we are not complete, we have not our accomplishment; but by both we have, and that fully, even by this day's royal exchange. Whereby, as before he of ours, so now we of his are made partakers. He clothed with our flesh, and we invested with his Spirit. The great promise of the Old Testament accomplished, that he should partake our human nature; and the great and precious promise of the New, that we should be *consortes divinae naturae*, 'partake his divine nature', both are this day accomplished.[5]

In the case of Lancelot Andrewes we have the benefit of the work of one of the very few Orthodox scholars who has made a detailed study of the Anglican tradition, Nicholas Lossky. In the articles which he has already published, Lossky has contributed much to our understanding of the consistently patristic nature of Andrewes' theology. This particular point illustrates its nature well. There is in Lancelot Andrewes nothing of that reticence towards the doctrine of *theosis* which is to be found in many Western theologians. Rather we find a renewal of the teaching of the Fathers in its fullness, a fullness which includes such themes as the constant progress into God described by St Gregory of Nyssa. In another sermon for Pentecost, Andrewes declares:

Now to be made partakers of the Spirit, is to be made partakers 'of the divine nature'. That is this day's work. Partakers of the Spirit we are, by receiving grace; which is nothing else but the breath of the Holy Ghost, the Spirit of grace. Grace into the entire substance of the soul, dividing itself into two streams; one goes to the understanding, the gift of faith; the other to the will, the gift of charity, the very bond of perfection. The tongues, to teach us knowledge; the fire, to kindle our affections. The state of grace is the perfection of this life, to grow still from grace to grace, to profit in it. As to go on still forward is the perfection of a traveller, to draw still nearer and nearer to his journey's end.[6]

With this remarkably dynamic definition of the state of grace, as constantly to grow, constantly to go forward, we may leave the work of Lancelot Andrewes, remarking only on its crucial significance in the life of the greatest English poet of our century, T. S. Eliot, who announced his return to the Christian faith in a little volume of essays which he published in

1928 entitled *For Lancelot Andrewes*, and whose understanding of the Christian faith, revealed above all in his *Four Quartets*, is deeply influenced by the vision of the seventeenth century bishop.

II

The theology of our Church as we find it in the seventeenth century is then a theology of the Incarnation, the Church and the Sacraments. It centres upon the thought of Christ as the head of redeemed humanity, of the Church as his body, of Christians as those who live in him, in the power of the Holy Spirit. During the eighteenth century this tradition grew weaker, though it never altogether disappeared and was expressed by the outstanding representative of our tradition in eighteenth-century America, Dr. Samuel Johnson of Connecticut (1696-1772) when he wrote: 'Christ was pleased now to tabernacle in our nature to save mankind, for he took not upon him the nature of angels, but the seed of Abraham, flesh of our flesh and bone of our bone, so as to be truly our head and representative to transact all affairs between God and us which concern our salvation.' The purpose of God's taking flesh was that we might be incorporate in Christ, 'so that by being united to our nature and dwelling in it, he is united to and dwells in us, and we in him. Thus by dwelling in the tabernacle of his Body, he has united himself to and dwells in mankind, especially in all the faithful, who are made members of his Body in baptism, and are partakers of his blessed body and blood in the holy Eucharist.'[7]

This whole vision of the nature of Christian life and faith and worship was reaffirmed with great force in the practice of nineteenth-century Anglicanism, in large measure on account of the movement of Church renewal which began in Oxford in 1833. It was a time of much church building, and of great pastoral activity. There was a rediscovery of the riches of the Church's tradition of liturgy and devotion. The Oxford movement grew out of a renewed faith in the saving reality of the Incarnation, with its double significance 'on the one hand that man's salvation comes from God alone; on the other, that God's saving action really penetrates and transforms man's world and man's life'.[8] The movement itself gave rise to new understandings of the implications of this doctrine, both for the inner life of man, and for life in its social and national dimensions.

From the renewal of sacramental life came a new vision of the Church's social apostolate, its mission to all humanity. There was implicit in the writings of Hooker and Andrewes a vision of the whole of life as sacramental, and an understanding that this general sacramentality was focussed in the sacraments of the Church—themselves derived from and expressing the mystery of the Incarnate Word, Christ himself, the great sacrament of God's wisdom and God's love. This vision was explicitly drawn out in relation to the new situations of the Church in a world of rapid social change, in the midst of the development of an industrial democracy. In particular the theme of the creation of man in the image of the Triune God was developed with a new urgency; the anthropological consequences of the doctrine of the Trinity became especially important.

We shall look at this theme in the work of theologians whose activity did not lie primarily in the universities, though the solid results of academic theology are presupposed in their teaching, but in the proclamation of the Church's message in the world of their time; in the work of men who may be said to have had a prophetic insight into the needs, personal and social, of Victorian England. In particular we shall look at the work of F. D. Maurice, perhaps the greatest Anglican theologian of the nineteenth century, and of one of his disciples, Thomas Hancock. We shall also consider the teaching of R. M. Benson, the founder of the oldest Anglican community for men, and certainly the outstanding monastic theologian of our Church since the Reformation. We shall notice in all these men a great desire to expound the Church's faith in God the Trinity, not as a matter of mere intellectual assent to a fixed dogmatic formula, but as a living apprehension of the reality of God himself, an apprehension in which we must become aware that it is we who are grasped by God before ever we can, in any sense, grasp him.

'The name of the Trinity,' writes F. D. Maurice, 'the Father, the Son and the Holy Ghost is, as the Fathers and Schoolmen said continually, the name of the infinite charity, of the perfect love, the full vision of which is that beatific vision for which saints and angels long even while they dwell in it.' To speak of God as Trinity is, for Maurice, to give substance to our faith that God is love. This is not a faith which Maurice accepted passively; it was one which he had gained through personal travail. His father was a Unitarian minister, and as a young man Maurice passed through a period of agnosticism. It was only in adult life that he was baptised into the Name of

8

the Father, the Son and the Holy Spirit. And this is a faith which for him not only declares the true nature of God; it also declares the true nature and calling of man. For all men are to be baptised into this Name, which is to unite the nations into one, 'by which men may be raised to the freedom and righteousness and fellowship for which they were created'. As Bishop Michael Ramsey comments in his valuable study of Maurice's teaching: 'Since the Triune God is the creator of the human race, the likeness of his eternal charity dwells in the human race, and the Trinity in Unity is the source of human fellowship in those who repent of their self-centred isolation and discover the true principle of their being.'[9]

This thought is given expression in a remarkable sermon of Thomas Hancock preached in 1869, with the title 'The Fellowship in God the Source of Humanity's Fellowship with God', the whole of which constitutes a powerful affirmation of faith in the living God of Scripture and Tradition:

> The human person through whom we have access to God is, the faith declares, God the Son. There is no certainty that God is the Father unless it be true that he has and ever has had, a co-eternal Son . . . St Hilary boldly said: 'We could not preach one God to men, if we had to preach a lonely God.' God is not merely *One*, not a mere unity, but he is the one *God*, that is, the one who is good, the one who includes in his perfect unity all possible good . . . The Divine Unity into whose Name the Son through whom we have access to that Unity commands us to baptise all nations and every creature is a Divine Unity; he is not a Divine solitariness, a Divine egotism . . . We ourselves deteriorate by the absence of fellowship, and we lose the power of drawing to us the faith and love and worship of others. God's revelation of himself to his human creatures as the Trinity in Unity—as Father, Son and Holy Ghost, one God—has drawn forth from men of all ages and places, of all degrees of culture and ignorance, the most wonderful joy, hope, faith and love. A man is at his highest, he is most perfectly a man, he is most godly, when he is living not as a mere unity, but as the fellow of a unity, as a kinsman in the family, as a citizen in the state, as a catholic in the Church, as a man in the human-kind . . . He who made us is not a cold, hard, lonely, self-amusing Mechanician, caring little what becomes of his experiments. In his being subsists the perfect Fellowship, the perfect Communion of which we have some imperfect shadow in our being, and for whose reproduction in us and our kind we crave with so insatiable a hunger.[10]

At every point Hancock, like his teacher Maurice, looks beyond the Church to the whole of humanity and the whole creation. He does this not because he regards the Church as of little importance, but because he believes that he who is the head of the Church is also, in some sense, the head of all humanity, the one in whom all men are to find their true destiny and calling.

> If we enter ever so little into the contemplation of the depths of the Catholic Faith—that is, the faith for all human kind and for every creature—we shall find it impossible to separate the unity of the Church from the unity of humanity; we shall find it impossible to separate the unity of humanity from the unity of God in Trinity. If we do not see that man's unity is in God, and that we can each enter into it in him, we shall seek it as the first violaters of the unity of mankind sought it, in some Tower of Babel—some colossal manufacture of human hands and brains.[11]

Here is a vision of the Church as the representative of all mankind gathered together in the power of the Spirit, called to participate in the very life of the Triune God. It was this understanding of things which forced Maurice himself, and all those whom he influenced, to look beyond the frontiers of the Church, to be concerned for the whole of human life. From the doctrines of the Incarnation and the Trinity, understood not as dead or abstract formulas, but as living and life-giving affirmations of faith and hope, they drew a whole programme of social action. Hancock in his own time was a prophetic voice, too little heeded. His outspoken denunciation of social and economic evils, taken together with the angularity of his character, prevented him from reaching a prominent position in the Church. He remained an assistant priest with no public status and very little recognition, one who was identified to an unusual degree with the hopes and aspirations of the industrial workers. But his theological vision was by no means his alone. He shared it with a whole group of men who had been inspired by the thought of F. D. Maurice. We find it again in a very different representative of the priesthood of the Church of England in the nineteenth century, Father R. M. Benson, the Superior and Founder of the Society of St John the Evangelist at Cowley in Oxford.

With Father Benson we face the mystery and the miracle of the restoration of spiritual gifts which had for long been neglected or ignored. For more than three hundred years there had been no monastic communities in the Church of England; now unexpectedly in the middle of the nineteenth century the gift of monastic life and monastic prayer was renewed. And with the gift of prayer and life there went, in the case of Benson, a gift of theology, understood much more in the sense in which the Fathers use that term than in the way in which it has commonly been used in the West in recent centuries . 'The use of the intellect is', he writes, 'that by knowing the things of God we may attain to the experimental knowledge of God's love. Otherwise our learning is only like a staircase leading to the top of a ruined tower.' And again: 'It is not enough for us to know what was fixed as the orthodox expression: we must have our minds trained affectionately in the orthodox consciousness, which is deeper and larger than the expression . . . by intellectual study we must gather up the teaching of past ages in the fullness of its scope. We have not to maintain truth, but to live in the truth so that it may maintain us.'[12]

Like F. D. Maurice, but I believe quite independently of him, the distinction between person and individual became for Father Benson of vital importance. When we speak of the individual we speak of man in his isolation, in his separateness, of man as competitor. When we speak of the person we speak of man in relationship, in communion, man as co-worker. If the life of the whole Church is in some sense a reflection or icon of the mystery of the Triune love, then the life of the community is to be so in a special way, for it is the purpose of the community 'to gather up and, as it were, focus the love which ought to animate the whole body of the Church Catholic.' We can see something of the way in which Benson taught if we consider this extract from an instruction given to his brethren in the first years of the community's life. We see how his teaching was at once very practical and deeply theological.

> Thy whole life must be a relative life. The moment thou art imprisoned in thine own self-consciousness, in thine own separate individuality, in the selfishness of thine own separated existence, thou committest a worse suicide than taking the life of thy body. Thou destroyest the very life of thy person. Thy person is a relative being and thou hast no existence save when thou actest for others. Man is created to be a social being. And as the Three Divine Persons have no life whatsoever except in this relativity of action, so we have no life whatsoever except in relative action towards others . . . It is the law of our nature that our life is personal, relative, communicating all that it has.

11

It is the law under which the Christian Church, the Body of Christ, is constituted. 'They had all things in common.' Property belongs to the dead world—community is the life of God.[13]

Remarkable words to come from the heart of nineteenth century England. As St Antony says, 'Your brother is your life.'

But, of course, it is not only in inter-personal relations that we come to know God. There is an inner journey of love and knowledge which leads us towards an ever-increasing entry into 'the dwelling places of the Three in One'. So it is not surprising that the doctrine of *theosis* is developed by Father Benson with remarkable emphasis. As a recent study of his Trinitarian theology concludes:

> Christian life, fully realised and lived, is nothing less than participation in the Divine life—it is *theosis*, deification . . . Constantly he uses the word 'deific' in its strict and full sense. He repeats the thought that it is 'into the Divine Life that we are gathered by our regeneration'; that we are 'made partakers of the Divine Nature', that 'we are called to participate in the uncreated energy of God'. His critique of nineteenth-century Christendom implies that the capacity to live the gospel authentically is entirely dependent on a vision of the unlimited resources of energy and love to which, in this deified relationship, the believer has access. The Christian life can be lived only when the Triune Life of God is 'felt as a power'.[14]

In the conjunction of pure theology with compassionate love for all men, there is an interesting parallel with St Calinic of Cernica, a contemporary of Father Benson and the most recently canonised saint of Romania. Father Benson, however, has not been widely read and it is only now, after almost a century, that the true importance of his theology, to which Archbishop Ramsey pointed more than thirty years ago, is beginning to be understood, and the relevance of his teaching to the twentieth century better appreciated.

III

We are brought back irresistably to the witness of the contemporary theologian with whom we began. David Jenkins also has a critique of our twentieth century Christendom, a Christendom in which our actions all too often give the lie to things which we affirm in our faith, so that orthodoxy is not always matched by orthopraxy or, to put it more simply, so that right thought is not always supported by right action. For David Jenkins, as for Benson, it is a failure of vision which lies at the root of our problems, a failure of vision 'of the unlimited resources of energy and love to which the believer has access, when the Triune Life of God is felt as a power'. Of course, Jenkins is facing a different set of problems from those which Father Benson faced a hundred years ago. The terms which he uses are often different. It is a testimony to the living nature of the tradition which he expresses that this should be so. To be true to the tradition is not primarily a question of repeating formulas. It is to live in communion with our fathers in the faith, sharing with them one vision and one life, the life which comes from God. It is to grow in the orthodox consciousness, which is deeper and larger than the orthodox expression. Not surprisingly for one who has worked and thought at the centre of the World Council of Churches, Jenkins is vividly aware of the many changes which are taking place in our world, changes at a spiritual level as well as at a social one: the shift of influence and initiative from Europe and North America to the countries of the Third World, the sudden enhancement of the position of women in society, the problems and the opportunities inherent in the process of rapid social change, the threat of violence, and the threat of war in our world situation.

As a theologian Jenkins is concerned to look in and through particular issues to the underlying features of the human situation, to seek for a renewal of vision of what it is to be man. He is sharply critical of the habit, particularly strong in the English-speaking countries, of looking only for 'pragmatic' solutions.

If we insist on being, as we call it, 'pragmatic' (or 'matter-of-fact') and refuse deeper reflection, disturbance or exploration, then we are bound to be treating human beings as simply 'things', that is, as nothing but an interesting collection of the *pragmata* from which the adjective 'pragmatic' derives. But human beings are not things, they are persons.

And in the Christian vision and understanding they are not even just historical persons (although they are at least that), they are potentially eternal persons.[15]

What is the nature of this vision? It is something very different from what we should call a 'mere theory', an intellectual abstraction with no necessary connection with life and experience. Rather it is something very close to the *theoria* of the Greek Fathers:

> . . . a practical and practising insight into a living mystery. For the word *theoria* was used, and needs to be revived, to refer to a spiritual capacity to develop insight into the vision and action of God, both beyond all things and through all things. This capacity is developed and deepened by the grace of God received through fellowship and the discipline of prayer, worship and a sustained pursuit of Christian discipleship in all things. Indeed, the spiritual capacity to see into and respond to the very heart and energy of things is the expression and experience of being in the image of God. It is because men and women are created by God in the image of God that they have the capacity to see and respond to him and to his energetic activities and possibilities in one another, in themselves and in all things.[16]

This consideration of man as created in God's image necessarily leads us to further reflection on the anthropological significance of the doctrine of the Trinity. But here an important point of terminology must be noted. Just as Christian *theoria* is far from being mere theory, so Christian doctrine is far from being merely intellectual and verbal. Jenkins prefers to speak of teaching about the Trinity as a symbol or icon:

> It has been the subject of much dotrinal discussion and reflects the insights gained and clarified in those discussions. But it operates as an articulated picture, with a worked out, recognised and traditional pattern which continues in use as a focus for and provocation of experience. The shape and pattern of this icon was worked out to present and represent a living possibility. This was (and is) glimpsed in images, words and actions. The whole process is kept alive by the activity the symbol reflects. Thus 'the Trinity' stands, not for doctrine, but for a way of life which is related to God's life.[17]

Thus to speak of the Holy Trinity is to speak of the immediacy and depth of the Church's apprehension of God as being at once immanent and transcendent. It is to speak of the particularity of his action in the flesh and blood of Jesus of Nazareth, and at the same time to affirm the universality of his action at all times and in all places. It speaks first

> of the over-ruling energy and presence of the transcendent God who is both the God of Israel and the God of the whole earth . . . secondly, of the historic energy and activity of Jesus, who he was, what he did and what was undergone by him and revealed through him in the episode of the cross and resurrection . . . thirdly, of the immanent activity of the Spirit continuing the story, developing the story, maintaining the knowledge of the story in actual communities and relating the implications of the story to living in touch with concrete realities.[18]

And a little further on Jenkins continues:

> Thus the symbol of the Trinity insists on and lays claim to a unique way of holding together transcendence and immanence, eternity and history, God and human beings. This, it proclaims, is the necessary and legitimate interpretation of the experienced and perceived story of God, Jesus and the Spirit, and of the story which therefore follows about God, men and the world. The dependent and temporary realities of nature and history, and of the conditions of human living within them, are in no way diminished as to their autonomy, authenticity and significance by the commitment of God to them and the involvement of God in them. At the same time God is neither defined nor limited by his unlimited involvement and his unambiguous commitment. He is Transcendence known to us as Transcendence in the midst.[19]

This is why in this vision of the Trinity we see the structure of supreme love, the affirmation of the reality of the presence of God's love in us and with us, that love which raises the dead and calls the things that are not into being and into life, that love which opens to men and women in all the limitations and fragility of their human existence, the infinite possibilities of the life and activity of God. 'Therefore it is clear that although God can be God without man and that God *is* God without man, none the less God *will not* be God without man. He does not need us. He loves us.'[20]

While it is certainly true that a single book by a single writer can hardly be taken to sum up the teaching of a whole theological tradition, it cannot be denied that this particular work, with its combination of a profound Chalcedonian orthodoxy in its exposition of the doctrines of the Incar-

15

nation and the Trinity, together with sensitive and perceptive awareness of the realities, spiritual and social, of our own day, represents in a remarkable way the latest growth of that tradition whose development we have sought to trace in this study. Taken together with Jenkins' earlier work, *The Glory of Man*, it offers us a striking testimony to the vitality of a theological position too often ignored in Western ecumenical debate.

CONCLUSION

What the importance of this theological tradition for the Eastern Orthodox will finally be is, of course, for the Orthodox themselves to say. They may well be inclined to ask how far it is possible to consider the theological position outlined here to be representative of Anglicanism as a whole when other writers could have been cited of different viewpoints who would also claim to speak on behalf of the Anglican Communion. The question is a real one. It is true that since the sixteenth century our tradition has contained within itself different schools of thought. Nevertheless, the Christological and Trinitarian emphases which characterise the writers we have quoted are, I believe, typical of that way of thought and teaching which is most central, most permanent and most significant in the history of our Church. On any showing, Hooker, Andrewes and Maurice would be acknowledged as three outstanding spokesmen of our position. That there are points of convergence between the position indicated here and the Orthodox tradition would seem sufficiently clear. How significant these similarities are is perhaps not yet wholly evident. For myself I must say that the parallels between the writers I have cited and representative Orthodox scholars seem very striking. In particular there are remarkable parallels with much that has been written in the renewal of Romanian Orthodox theology in the last thirty years, and one is led to wonder whether, in addition to the general affinity of Anglican with Orthodox, there is a specific relationship between English and Romanian theology due in part to the mediating positions held by our two nations. These are questions which deserve to be further investigated. One point which it is interesting to note is that while all the authors quoted in this paper were familiar with the writings of the Fathers, at least with those of the first five centuries, none except David Jenkins had any direct theological contact with their Eastern Orthodox contemporaries. If there are real points of agreement they have been reached through fidelity to common origins, not through direct influence or imitation.

16

From the Anglican side I am convinced that the fuller and more conscious recognition of our relationship to Orthodoxy is of crucial importance for the future of our tradition. The encounter with Orthodoxy can provide us with a key which enables us to understand the development of that tradition in a new and more coherent way. The *via media* which our Church has always sought to preserve since the break with Rome is no longer seen as a mere compromise, but as an attempt to witness in the West to a fullness and a balance of the faith which Orthodoxy has always preserved in the East. What I should like to ask my Orthodox colleagues is whether the encounter with Anglicanism, not only in its contemporary representatives but in its outstanding spokesmen during the last four centuries, may not provide them with a clue to finding new ways to expound and live their faith in a world which has been so largely shaped by ideas and forces coming from the West. I have sometimes the feeling that it has been given to the Churches of the Anglican Communion to prepare a place in which in the West, the faith and life of Orthodoxy may find its own roots, its hitherto unacknowledged Western tradition. At all events I am very sure that in a world which has suddenly become one, not only at an economic but also at a spiritual level, the old distinctions of East and West have very largely ceased to be meaningful. It is in a new realisation of the unity of all mankind in the providence and love of the Triune God, Father, Son and Holy Spirit, that we are all being called together at the present time.

NOTES

1   David Jenkins, *The Contradiction of Christianity*, (SCM Press 1976), p.145.

2   Richard Hooker, *The Laws of Ecclesiastical Polity*, ed. John Keble, (Oxford 1836) Book V, ch.1.3, p.218.

3   Ibid. V, ch. lvi. 7, p. 249.

4   C. S. Lewis, *English Literature in the Sixteenth Century* (Oxford 1954), pp.459-461.

5   Lancelot Andrewes, *Complete Works*, Library of Anglo-Catholic Theology (Oxford, 11 Vols. 1841-54) Vol. III, pp.108-9.

6   Ibid. p.367.

7   Louis Weil, 'Worship and Sacraments in the Teaching of Samuel Johnson of Connecticut'. Unpublished doctoral thesis at the Institut Catholique in Paris, 1972, pp.146-7.

8   E. R. Fairweather (ed.), *The Oxford Movement* (New York 1964), p.11.

9   A. M. Ramsey, *F. D. Maurice and the Conflicts of Modern Theology* (London 1951), pp.54-55.

10 Quoted in A. M. Allchin, *The Spirit and the Word: Two Studies in Nineteenth Century Anglican Theology* (London 1963), pp. 55-57.

11 Ibid. p.60.

12 R. M. Benson *Followers of the Lamb* (Oxford 1905), pp. 10-11.

13 From the MS volume of the Retreat of July 1874, at Cowley.

14 See the article by Martin Smith SSJE in *Christian*, Vol.4, No.1 (Epiphany 1977) p.24.

15 David Jenkins, *The Contradiction of Christianity* (see note 1), p.99.

16 Ibid. p.100.

17. Ibid. p.143.

18 Ibid. p.150.

19 Ibid. p.157.

20 Ibid. p.157.